Fly Fishing for PANFISH

BY
JOE BRUCE

Copyright © 1998 Joe Bruce

Published by K&D Limited, Inc.
14834 Old Frederick Road
Woodbine, MD 21797
410-489-4967

Printed in the United States of America

All rights reserved. No part of this book may be used or reproduced in any manner whatsoever without written permission from the author. A reviewer may quote brief passages.

ISBN 0-9637161-3-1

Library of Congress Cataloging-in-Publication Data
Bruce, Joe, 1946 -
    Fly fishing for panfish : a mini-book / by Joe Bruce.
       p. cm.
    ISBN 0-9637161
    1. Fly fishing. 2. Panfish fishing. I.Title
SH456.B7235 1997
799.1'24--dc21   97-13391
                                      CIP

Photos by author.
Cover and text design by Donna J. Dove, K&D Limited, Inc.

Contents

	Acknowledgements	5
	Preface	6
	Foreword	8
Chapter 1	About Panfish	11
	Bluegill	14
	Crappie	17
	Yellow Perch	19
Chapter 2	Tackle	23
	Rods	23
	Reels	26
	Lines	27
	Leaders	30
	Knots	32
Chapter 3	Flies and Patterns	39
	Surface Patterns	40
	Sub-surface Patterns	49
	Bottom Bouncers	56
Chapter 4	Fishing Techniques	69
	Where to Fish	69
	Tides and Brackish Water	74
	Surface Fishing	76
	Sub-surface	79
	Bottom-Bouncing	86
Chapter 5	Panfish Through the Seasons	91
	Winter	91
	Spring	92
	Summer	92
	Fall	93
	Conclusion	95

To Fred,
My favorite panfish partner. . . I miss you.

Acknowledgements

Satisfied customers are a necessity for any retail business, and a fly shop is certainly no exception. I *must* attract customers if my shop, *The Fisherman's Edge*, is to be successful. People come into the shop for all kinds of reasons. Some are travelling in the area and see the address in the phone book, some stop in when they accidentally pass the store, some see an ad, and some may have read an article I've written. Fortunately, many come in because they have been referred by other customers.

These people look over the merchandise, swap stories, and ask advice. Some just pass through, but often a nice thing happens, and some stay and become "regulars."

These regulars are people who I consider to truly be my friends, and I sincerely hope the feeling is mutual. We have coffee together, share a lunch, laugh and talk for hours (I'm seldom at a loss for words), and we occasionally go out to dinner. We go on fishing trips together; sometimes for the day and sometimes on extended out-of-state trips. Sometimes they come in to buy things, but often they will just drop in to say "Hi."

You really are my friends, and I wish to thank all of you for enriching my life!

PREFACE

Do you remember when you were a kid, those first few mornings in the summer when you awoke with a start? "I'm late for school," flashed through your mind. Then you realized that the school year had ended and you didn't have any more school until fall. What a great feeling. I would lay back on my bed and start thinking, "I bet the sunfish are biting at the pond." With that thought, there would be no more possibility of sleeping; there were fish waiting and my excitement level would have me wide awake.

Those memories are from well over forty years ago, and I still get the same thrill today when I think about fishing for panfish. Although I have fished for more glamorous fish like bonefish and tarpon, my love for panfish has never diminished.

Every spring will find me on my favorite lake or pond, looking for these feisty fish. They are my roots; they were the first fish that I caught on a fly rod. They helped me learn to fly fish, and they have continued to teach me many things over the years. For either the novice or advanced fly fisher, these willing fish can teach you techniques and skills that will help you later when you're seeking some of their larger cousins.

The following pages reflect my many years, along with some of my fishing companions' experiences, of fishing for these miniature gamefish. We will concentrate on the three most sought-after panfish: bluegill, crappie and yellow perch.

Many of the fly patterns that we'll cover are of my design or incorporate my modifications to existing patterns. You will find that quite a few of these fly patterns can be used for other fish species. Some flies are from other fly tiers and fishermen who have generously let me share their work in the hope that our collective experience can make your fishing as rewarding as ours has been.

This book is part of a series of books on flies and fishing techniques for various fish species. The series is intended to serve as a source of "getting started" information about fly fishing for species "beyond" trout. Both the novice and the advanced fly-fisher will find plenty of useful information. I want to help you see new ways of looking and thinking about ways to fish, and about the fish themselves. I hope some of the information in this book will make you feel the same way about panfish as I do. I'm a kid again on these fishing days. I hope they can make you feel like one too.

Good luck, and have fun fishing!

Joe with a colorful yellow perch.

FOREWORD

Shortly before this book was to go to print, my son, Rick, showed me this reminiscence he had written. I thought it so fitting that I asked him if I could include it, and he graciously agreed. I hope you like it as much as I do!

Farm Pond Panfish

by Rick Bruce

Only the slightest breeze drifted across the fields surrounding the small farm pond, causing the cattails to shimmer and dance to the frog's evening chorus. The sun, slowly making its way to its resting place, set the horizon ablaze in fiery orange and red.

It had been three years since my last visit to the water's edge, but its magic and beauty still had not faded. I took in the smell of the crisp fall air, the Canadian geese bedding down on the far shore, and the small dimples that formed on the water's surface as the pond's inhabitants rose up to pluck a quick evening meal. They all reminded me of the many times in my youth my father and I would come here to enjoy the brilliant transition from day to night. Even my fly rod brought back memories of days long past. It had been my father's rod, given to me on my fifteenth birthday. Nothing glamorous or fancy, but to me the rod held more value than if it had been cast of solid gold. With solemn reverence, I threaded the line through its well-worn guides, tied on a tiny yellow popper and stripped out enough line to attempt my first cast.

A few quick motions and the fly line gracefully unfurled across the pond's mirrored surface, the small ripples in its wake warping the reflected sunset into a kaleidoscope of color. The popper sat but for a moment before a slight tug revealed the sunfish had discovered my evening offering. With each tiny pull on the line, the fly tempted the fish, threatening them with an opportunity lost should they let it escape. This evening it was a threat for which they would not stand.

The second strike could not be called a tug, for it likened much more to the blow of a well-placed hammer. With a rapid jerk, the tiny hook set firmly in the bluegill's jaw. Valiantly, my adversary struggled against its ensnarement, darting first left only to quickly reverse course in a desperate charge for the cattails. Only barely was I able to turn the fight back to deeper water before he entangled me in the reeds.

Another minute, and the contest was over. Gingerly, I unhooked my gallant foe and gently returned him to his watery home. As he slipped back into the depths, I was reminded of why I come back to this forgotten pond. Ounce for ounce, none fights so mightily as the magnificent little panfish.

FLY FISHING FOR PANFISH

Chapter 1

ABOUT PANFISH

This book will describe how to catch the three most sought-after fresh water panfish in the United States: bluegill, crappie, and yellow perch. Although there are many species of panfish, the techniques and flies we'll describe will work for all the other varieties as well. In fact, we'll even talk a little bit about brackish and tidal water fishing just to make sure all techniques for these little dynamos are well covered.

There are no fish that have made a novice fisherman happier than the panfish. Bluegill, crappie, yellow perch, etc. are the fish that most people "cut their teeth on." From the little community ponds to the large lakes and rivers, you will find there are panfish. These fish are almost anxious to allow you to perfect your angling skills, whether you're fishing on the surface or underneath. The

A few fish and all you need to catch them.

experience that you will gain from tackling these feisty fish will go a long way in helping you handle larger fish on the fly rod. Throwing a popping bug to bluegill, and having them explode on the surface, is a thrill that I have looked forward to for over thirty-five years and I'm always waiting for the first opportunity in the early spring to hook up with some of these fine fish. Can you imagine if bluegill always got to be three or four pounds? We might not ever fish for anything else! These scrappy, hard fighting fish seem always willing to bite... *sometimes*. Although these panfish are associated with freshwater, they are all just as much at home in brackish water.

Joe with a handsome crappie.

ABOUT PANFISH

Late winter and early spring will find my panfish box stuffed full of black wooly buggers.

All three species are also forage fish for the larger predatory fish that roam the waters which they inhabit. The yellow perch are the slowest growing, and because of this are a food source for a longer period of time than the faster growing bluegill and crappie. To offset this slow growth the perch has a very high rate of survival from the egg.

Crappie and yellow perch in the springtime are also great fare on the fly rod. Catching crappies in the 12-inch range on a light fly rod (and the same with yellow perch), sure can turn a cool spring day into a much warmer one in the heart as well as the body. Early spring also has a certain air about it with the birds singing and nesting and the first wild flowers starting to bloom. Add a healthy dose of panfish and you can't help but be rejuvenated.

Although these fish are smaller in stature than the more glamorous gamefish, they are a fish that will enhance and accelerate your ability to fish with the fly rod. *Never look down on them.*

Fish for these rascals on a three- or four-weight outfit and they will put a bend in your rod just like tarpon or bonefish will on a heavier rod.

How did panfish get their name? We can only assume that the word refers to how nicely they can be cooked up in a frying pan. I hardly feel it's the shape of a monstrous bluegill, which sometimes is referred to as a dinner plate with lips. Let's take a closer look at our three featured species.

Bluegill

Let's look first at the king of the sunfishes. No, I'm not referring to the largemouth bass, although they do belong to the sunfish species. I'm talking about the bluegill, known (along with other small sunfish) in the Southern States as *bream* (pronounced "brim"). These fish offer something for everybody. They are generally willing to bite and they are usually found in great numbers. They range from 2 inches to 10 inches, but the average size is more near the 6-inch mark. They can live to a ripe old age of eleven years, but closer to nine is probably average.

A bluegill at the surface.

ABOUT PANFISH

Barb with one of her many bluegill catches.

    The bluegill is the best known of the sunfishes, but there are countless other sunfish species around the United States (just a few you may have heard of are banded sunfish, green sunfish, long-ear sunfish, red-ear sunfish and spotted sunfish). Bluegills are usually the first fish that most budding fishermen catch, be it on spinning rods or fly rods. Their sheer numbers in lakes and ponds make them a perfect first-fish quarry. Would you believe the world record bluegill weighed a whopping 4 pounds, 12 ounces? It was caught in Ketona Lake, Alabama in 1950. Is this still a panfish? Imagine the size of the pan needed to fry that one up.

    Spawning begins in spring when the waters warm to about 68 degrees. The nests are generally in a depth of 2 to 4 feet of

Bill Kollmer will fly fish for panfish every chance he gets.

water and are guarded by the male bluegill after the eggs are laid. Working these beds with a popping bug can sometimes provide nonstop action. In some clear lakes the beds can be down in the 10- to 12-foot level. Here is where the largest bluegill spawn. They can be tough to reach with a fly rod, not so much because of the depth, but because they generally will put their nests around and in between downed trees and logs. Large bluegill are no dummies. Some people think that these fish *always* bite. I guarantee you that is not the case.

ABOUT PANFISH

Bluegill can be caught all year around, with spring, summer and fall being the best and in that order of success. Winter "gilling" can be tough, but doable. Extremely slow retrieves with sinking lines will usually cure some "cabin fever."

Food sources for bluegill will run the gamut from small larva to crustaceans to small minnows. Because of this variety of food, they can be caught on wet flies, dry flies, nymphs and streamers.

Bluegill as well as crappie and yellow perch are all structure oriented. They need cover to ambush food, to provide a place to rest and give protection from larger predators. Structure can consist of trees in the water, brushes, rock piles, underwater roots, overhangs or man-made structures like dams, bridges, piers, etc.

Crappie

Crappie have had more names dropped on them than any other species alive. Some of their fifty or so names are calico bass, specks, speckled perch, papermouths, and strawberry bass. As table fare, these fish need not take a back seat to any other. They are

A fine crappie just before being released.

avidly pursued by the vast majority of freshwater fisherman for whom fishing is a food source.

There are two species of crappie, the white and the black, and both species can sometimes be caught in the same waters. There are two ways to tell them apart. The first one is absolute. The black crappie has seven to eight dorsal spines and the white crappie only six. The second difference sometimes can be a little harder to identify because of water coloration and the structure that the fish are inhabiting at the time. The white crappie usually has black to dark olive spots made up in vertical bars on their sides, whereas the black crappie's spots are scattered over the body.

Black crappie are strictly carnivorous, feeding on small fish, aquatic insects and crustaceans throughout their life, whereas the white crappie will feed on aquatic insects and plankton when they are small; but when they are larger, they'll feed mostly on fish.

Both species spawn in late spring. They are not great nest builders. They spend little time in preparing a bed. Their nest can be in an opening in the grass or in areas around stumps or roots near shore. The male white crappie will guard the nest, much like sunfish, whereas neither the male nor female black crappie will stay near its nest.

Crappie tend to have population cycles. They range from a dominant group in some years to only a few fish being caught in others. There can be a massive group of crappie in a given water for two to three years and then they'll almost disappear for the same time span. This group will spawn and eat their offspring (as well as any other forage fish) for this period until there are not very many crappie left. Then the boom cycle will start up again. Life expectancy for both species is around six years.

They can become sizeable even with their short life span. The world record white crappie tipped the scales at 5 pounds, 3 ounces, and was caught at Enid Dam, Enid Lake, Mississippi in

A nice yellow perch... panfish can be caught throughout the seasons; note the gloves.

1957. The record black crappie came from Kerr Lake in Virginia in 1981. It weighed 4 pounds, 8 ounces.

Yellow Perch

The yellow perch is another of the panfish with a few nicknames. Ringed perch, striped perch, and coon perch are a few. These names refer to the yellow perch's most distinguishing features, the vertical bars found on its body. The body usually has a golden yellow coloration, but I have caught yellow perch in Canada's Ontario Province that had a red body color. This one is hard to figure out, as there was no evidence of red-colored insect life on the bottom, or any red coloration on rocks or vegetation.

The yellow perch is generally considered a cold water species, being catchable in the cooler months. There is some justification to this thinking, since they don't live much farther south

Joe showing that he is a happy man.

than a line drawn from South Carolina westward. They extend northward to the southern portions of West-Central Canada and to Nova Scotia.

The yellow perch is a slow-growing fish, only reaching a length of about six and a half inches in three years. Because of this, they are a forage fish to the larger predatory fish for that time period. But nature takes care of this by giving the females the ability to lay an egg mass that can total from 10,000 to 75,000 eggs, out of which there is a twenty to forty percent survival rate of the fry the first year. Spawning takes place in late winter or early spring, when the water temperature reaches between 43 to 50 degrees. There is no parental protection. The fry survive by eating zooplankton and insect larva, and as they grow they will eat insects, crayfish, fish eggs and fry.

As stated, they are slow growing, but can live as long as eleven years. The world record is one of the oldest. A 4 pound, 3 ounce yellow perch was caught in the Delaware River, New Jersey, in 1865.

The yellow perch is at home in clear freshwater lakes as well as in brackish water. They are found in the saltwater tributaries and not usually in the larger bays or estuaries unless the salt content is low. Here in our Chesapeake Bay they are only found in the tributaries and not in the Bay proper, although they will occasionally move there after large storms have pumped vast amounts of freshwater into the Bay. Perch tend to live out their lives in the same body of water they were born in, unless they are redistributed by storms.

FLY FISHING FOR PANFISH

Chapter 2

TACKLE

Rods

Ultralight or light fly rods are the right choice for panfish. What are "ultralights?" Let me relate it to spin-fishing, since most people have at least some experience with spinning gear. Spin rods are classified as ultralight, light, medium and heavy. Generally the first spin rod that a budding fisherman buys is a medium action rod. This rod has the most versatility; it will use line testing anywhere from six to twelve pounds, will accommodate lure weights from 1/8 to 3/8 of an ounce, and will be from six to seven feet long. This will handle the vast majority of fish, from panfish to largemouth bass. The spin fisherman who enjoys panfish will eventually move to an ultralight spin rod, because these lighter rods will allow greater fight from the fish. In other words, you size your tackle to the fish. Line weights will run from two- to four-pound test, and lure weights from 1/32 to 1/4 ounce. These rods will be six feet or under in length.

Rods for fly fishing run from two weights to twelve weights. Fly lines are classified by size according to the weight of the first 30 feet, measured in grains. In fly fishing, it is the weight of the *line* which carries the fly through the air (wind resistance is a determining factor; big flies, heavy rods). In spinning it is the weight of the *lure* which carries the line through the air. You choose a spin rod based on the weight of the lure you are intending to throw. You wouldn't cast a four-ounce lure on an ultralight rod; you would look to a heavier rod to accomplish this. With fly rods we have the

Good panfish gear. . . 3- to 6-weight fly rods, floating and sink-tip lines and a good assortment of flies.

same situation: two and three weights are the "ultralights," twelve weights are heavy gear, and six weights fall into the medium range. *Panfish rods will use line weights from two to six.*

Since most panfishing tends to be in open water, fly rods from 8-1/2 feet to 10 feet long are the best choices. The nine-foot rod is probably the standard in the market. The longer length will allow longer casts. Considering that all rods are levers, if you increase the length of the lever, you can do more work; so, longer rods will give you more distance with less effort. Of course, additional rod length isn't the "silver bullet" for better casting. Good casting practices start at home, not on the water. Learn the fundamentals of the cast so that when you are on the water, you can be relaxed and can concentrate on fishing, not casting. Casting is the foundation of fly fishing, and learning it shouldn't be rushed. Read about the mechanics of the basic cast and practice them — and then practice some more. This time is not wasted; even the best casters continue to practice their routine. If you are having problems with your technique, seek out help; most fly shops can help you with your casting.

If you already fly fish, then by all means start with whatever rod you have; the fish don't care, they haven't read this book. If you are just getting started and are only getting one rod, then pick up a five- or six-weight outfit in an 8-1/2 to 9-foot length. This mid-size set-up will do the most for you, since it's not too heavy for panfish, yet you can use it on other species as well. Fly rods have different types of actions, usually described as fast, moderate or slow. These actions refer to where the rod bends when it's under a load. The fast action rod will bend nearer the tip, and the slow action will bend clear down into the handle of the rod. Which action is best for you? *It's the one which you feel most comfortable with and can cast best.* Even if you are not yet a good caster, one style of rod will reinforce your casting ability. There is *no substitute* for actually trying out rods. Don't fall into the trap of automatically using the one that your fishing buddy recommends. Your casting style and your buddy's style could be different (in fact, they probably are), making his recommendation the wrong one for you. Try all the rods you can get your hands on, in the line weight that you want, and make your judgment based on your own experience. If it is your first rod I encourage you to buy it from a shop that you have confidence in. A reputable fly shop won't steer you wrong; they want you as a customer for the long haul. Like with spinning gear, you eventually will own more than one fly rod.

Most fly shops have start-up kits that are either factory set-ups or start-up outfits that the shop has put together. In either case these are usually matched for the correct balance of rod, line and reel. You *do* want to buy a "balanced" outfit.

Reels

If you have a trout-sized fly outfit, then you probably have the right reel. If you are buying one for the first time, then a little education might be helpful. Panfish don't necessarily warrant a top-of-the-line reel, but try to buy the best that you can afford. This advice goes for all the gear that you may purchase down the road. Better equipment will last longer and can be the right gear when you're pursuing other bigger and stronger gamefish.

Generally, reels fall into three manufacturing styles: plates and pillars, cast, or machined from bar stock aluminum. The plates and pillars style is the least expensive. They are constructed by making front and rear plates which are separated by hollow tubes with long bolts and nuts connecting the plates. These reels have entirely too many parts; eventually a nut or bolt will work loose and ruin your fishing for the day. If you can avoid these fly reels, by all means do so.

The next type, cast reels, tend to be good entry level reels. Cast reels are made in sizes for every line weight. Some are injected-molded under pressure, creating (if properly designed) the same tensile strength as reels cut from bar stock aluminum. Some are made with removable plastic cassettes to be used in place of additional spools (which can be costly). With this system it's easy to carry several spools of different lines at a cost per spool of around ten dollars. Cast reels are manufactured for companies like Cortland Line Company, STH, Orvis and Scientific Angler. Prices for a panfish size reel run from around $35 to $145 and everything in between.

The next class of reels are the premium models. They are machined from blocks of aircraft-grade bar stock aluminum, and are very light in weight for their size. Great emphasis is placed on precision tolerances between spool and reel housing and in all other milled parts. These reels have the most elaborate drag systems,

TACKLE

Lines for panfishing from top-water to "bottom-bouncing."

with a goal of durability and smoothness — especially in the start-up when motion first begins. They are the "cream of the crop," and their price tags will reflect it. However, like any well made equipment, they will last you a fishing lifetime. Are they *needed* for panfishing? No, but if you feel strongly about having the best gear, they may be for you.

Lines

When you're buying lines, you don't want to skimp on cost. Better lines are better lines. They float better and they last longer. They have harder finishes, reducing friction of the line through the rod guides. This allows more distance with less energy exerted. They will not pick up as much microscopic dirt particles as a cheaper line. Their harder finish won't allow dirt to get into the pores of the line. They will not get as sticky or as limp under the heat of the summer sun, and will "shoot" through the guides better. There will be no sagging between the guides. Again, better lines *are* better lines. Good lines cost from $40 to $60 and will last the average fly fisherman three to five years. Not a bad investment for the amount of time you'll use them and the pleasure you'll get from them.

What lines do you need for panfishing? There are three of them. *You will need a weight-forward floating line, a short sink-*

A small boat or canoe is all that's needed to put you in good panfish waters.

TACKLE

tip (5' to 10') and long sink-tip or a full sinking line. These will cover 95% or more of panfishing situations, whether in a lake or pond, brackish water or in saltwater for yellow perch.

Let's briefly look at each line. Their uses will be explained in more detail in Chapter 4, when we discuss fishing techniques. The *weight-forward floating* line will take care of surface action using poppers or dry flies for bluegill. Also, this line can be used when the crappie (in the lakes) are dimpling the surface. They probably are taking emerging insects just under the surface.

The next line should be your "bread & butter" line for shallow water fishing, and it is the *5- or 10-foot sink-tip.* This is the line of choice in either fresh or saltwater when fishing in less than four feet of water. These lines can be bought in different sink rates for the ten-foot tips, but the five-foot sink-tips only come in one sink rate of about 6 inches to 6-1/2 inches per second. Two line manufacturers make the sink-tips. Cortland Line Co. makes line weights from 5-weight up, and Teeny Nymph Lines make them from 3-weight and up. As for the 10-foot lines, buy the fastest sink rate you can get; you can use your retrieve to adjust the sink rate. The faster you retrieve the line the less chance the line has to sink, since the floating portion tends to pull the sinking line to the surface. You have to be careful, though, as too quick a retrieve reduces the time the fly travels in the holding area where the fish are.

The final line you'll need is either a *full-sinking line or a long sink-tip* of about 20 feet. Our experience says that the long sink-tip will get the job done most of the time. If the fish you are after are deeper than twenty feet, there are better fishing tools. Waiting forty seconds or longer to allow the fly line to get to that depth is not what I call a good time. Fishing the line to twelve or fifteen feet, at maximum, is a better range for the fly rod. Fishing any deeper would require setting an anchor if you were fishing from a boat. By the time the line could sink that far, there would be a strong chance that any little breeze would push you off the area you were intending to fish. From the shore you have another problem. The bank slopes down into the water, and your line will be following the same route up as it is retrieved. Chances are, you will get snagged long before you can get the line up. These sinking lines tend to sink with a belly in them, meaning that somewhere out there a portion of the line has sunk faster, causing it to reach the bank slope first. In general this type of line is best fished out of a water craft or, if wading, by casting either diagonally or parallel to the shoreline. Don't be misled by any potential difficulties; this is a line that you shouldn't be without. When the fish are deep, this *is* the right fly line to reach them.

Leaders

Leaders aren't complex for panfish. A leader for the floating line should be from 7-1/2' to 9' long, tapered down to a six to eight pound (4x and 3x diameter) tippet. The sinking lines are even

An assortment of leaders and spools of tippet.

TACKLE

A must for a lot of us fly guys... a stripping basket to keep the line from under your feet or anything else in the boat.

simpler. Take about three to four feet of six or eight pound test tippet material, and you're in business. This short leader allows the fly to get down to the strike zone with the line. Fishing a longer leader will defeat this. Monofilament tends to float, which will cause the fly to rise up off the bottom. The intent of using a sinking line is to get the fly down with it. This short tippet near the fly line won't deter the take. Fish are not alarmed by something long and dark in the water. How many twigs, branches, grasses do you think a fish sees in its lifetime? Your fly line is just another one.

Their interest would more likely be in any food that is clinging to the clear weed. Now, mind you, I have never been told by a fish that this is the case, but if they were alarmed by every thing that ever floated past them, they would never eat. I have sometimes fished this tippet as short as 12" because I was too lazy to change it. If you're catching fish, it's hard to make yourself take the time to change to a longer one.

Knots

We are not going to tell you how to tie specific knots at this point, since there are plenty of books on the subject available. Often, there will be a few useful examples in the pamphlets that came with your fly lines. The one thing to remember is *to tie good knots.* A correctly tied knot will always perform better than a badly tied one. If you don't feel the knot that you just tied isn't a good one, then retie it. You never know when that fish of a lifetime will hit your fly. You will feel pretty bad if you know you lost the fish due to a simple factor that was totally under your control.

Another thing to keep in mind when you're out there and catching a mess of bluegill or crappie is that the knot is still the weakest link between you and the fish. A knot that has been subjected to fish's teeth, snags, and encounters with the bottom has less than the 100% knot strength that it had when you first tied the fly on. So, after a bout with all these things, take the time to sit down and retie that fly back on with a new, fresh knot. This just makes good common sense. We *know* we should do this, but I'll bet you are like me: "Just one more fish and I'll re-tie. Honest."

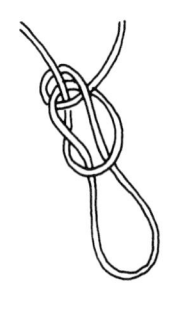

Perfection Loop

There are only a few knots needed to handle fly fishing gear, and some you probably already know. The first one is the connection between the fly reel arbor and the backing.

Surgeon's Loop

I prefer to make a *perfection* or *surgeon's loop* knot, loop the standing part of the line through it, and throw this over the spool to form a *clove hitch*. On some reels where the spool is not easily removed you can use an *arbor knot*. After winding on the backing, you need to make a decision. Do you attach the fly line to the backing with a permanent knot or do you form a loop in the backing and form a loop in the end of the fly line and attach these together with a "*loop-to-loop*" fastening. Either method is fine. If you decide to make a permanent knot, tying the backing

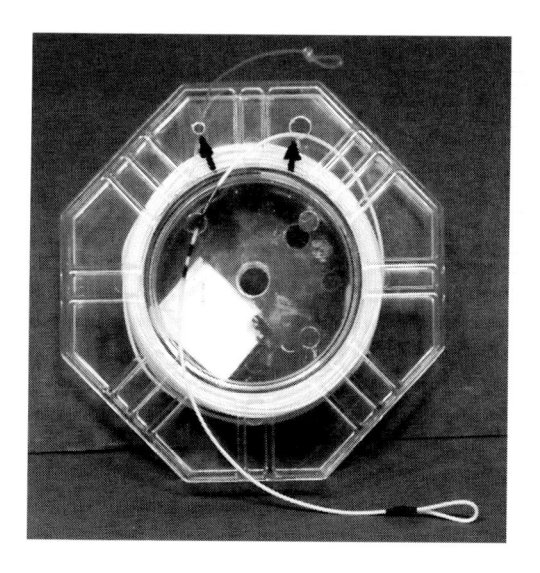

A fly line spool set up as a storage container for your additional lines. Note arrows showing holes in the spool for your leader and end of fly line that attaches to your backing.

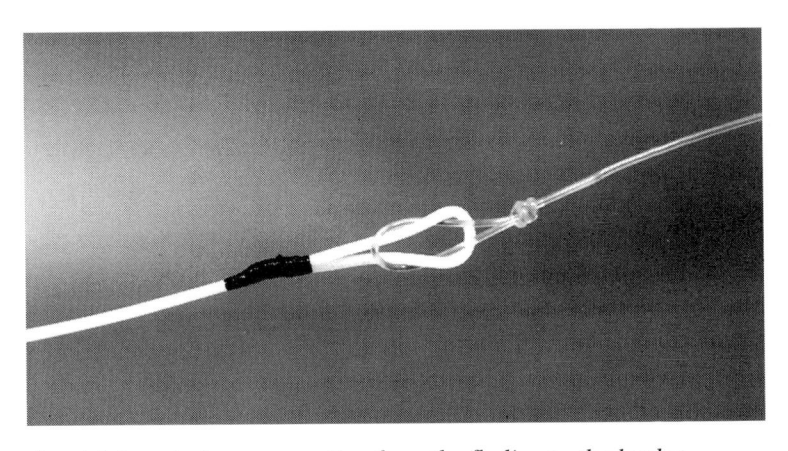

A quick loop-to-loop connection from the fly line to the leader.

to the fly line with a *nail knot* is fine for lines under six weight. If you decide to use the *loop-to-loop* method, tie a *surgeon's loop* in the backing large enough to encompass the line spool that came with your fly line. The added bonus of doing this type of connection is that you can now change whole fly lines without the added expense of extra reel spools. This is not a fast-change operation and it does require you to carry the line spool that came with your fly line to contain your spare line. The advantage is that it will save some money if this appeals to you. If so, take the line spool and glue the two halves together (if it comes apart when you have line stored on it, you can have a real mess on your hands). This will be your storage container for changing lines. Drill two holes in the spool on one side. Make one small hole for the leader and a larger one for the loop that will be on the back end of the fly line. Now you simply have to insert the leader in the small hole and start winding the fly line on the spool. When you reach the connection between the fly line and backing, insert the line spool through the large backing loop and insert the fly line loop through the larger hole in the spool and you're ready to wrap another line on the fly reel.

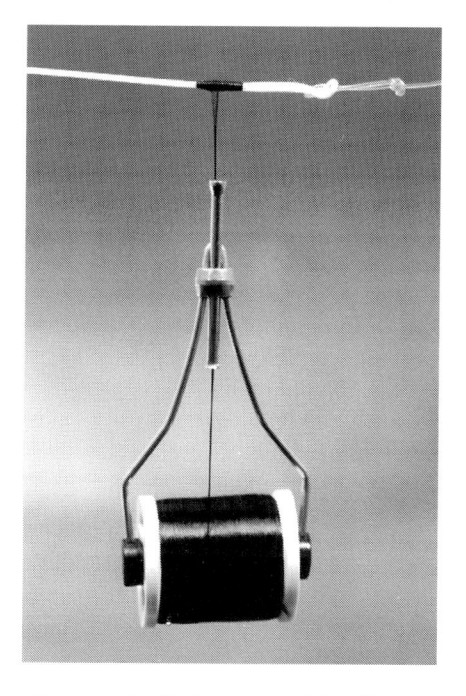

Forming the fly line loop with a fly tying bobbin.

To use this system you will, of course, have to form a loop in the fly line. This is accomplished by looping back about 3/4" of fly line on to itself and *whipping* thread around this loop. A fly-tying bobbin which holds rod-winding thread is a great help for making this connection. After whipping the tag end of the material, cover the knot with a knot dressing like "Pliobond" or "Loon Knot Sense." The latter is much faster to work with. I use the Loon dressing for any knot which I feel needs to be coated.

After the fly line and backing are attached you will need to make the transition from the fly line to the leader. A twelve inch piece of thirty pound stiff monofilament constructed to form a *butt loop* will make this connection. Fasten one end of the stiff mono

I always use a non-slip loop knot to create more animation in my fly or popper.

to the fly line with a *nail* knot. Put a loop in the other end with either a *perfection loop* or a *double surgeon's knot.* Put a loop in the other end of your leader and use a *loop-to-loop* connection to fasten the leader to the *butt loop*. The only knot left is the connection between the leader and the fly. I prefer to use the *"non-slip" loop* here. This simple but strong knot will let your fly move and swing around during the retrieve, allowing more animation in your presentation. I have a theory that the knot has the added bonus of looking like a small scud or shrimp that the fly is chasing. The segments on the knot above the fly tend to have the look of the segments on these crustaceans. This chase scenario helps trigger the predator strike by giving the fish the illusion that, for the same effort, it can get two meals. Remember, this is only a theory, the fish have *not yet* talked to me about it, but anything that can boost your confidence in what you are doing will put more fish on your line; and I have confidence that this works.

TACKLE

Need help with these knots? Most good fly shops will do them for you during the purchase of the outfit or at least will show you how to tie these knots. They aren't hard, they just need to be practiced to be perfected and remembered.

FLY FISHING FOR PANFISH

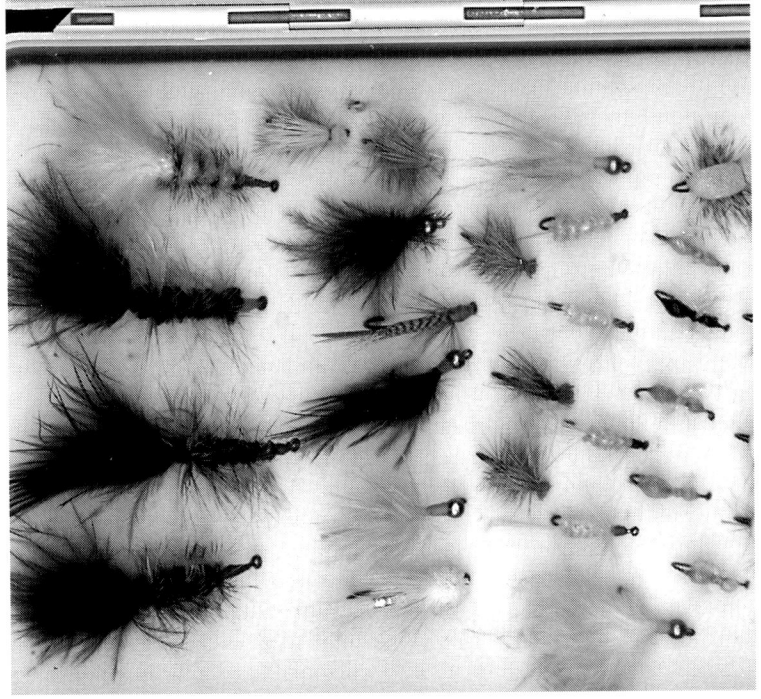

Chapter 3

FLIES AND PATTERNS

Let's look at some of the fly patterns that have proven successful for panfish. They will cover water depths from top to bottom (note that we've divided the sections into surface patterns, sub-surface patterns, and bottom-bouncers). Some patterns will be better for one species, whereas others will be good for all three. Some are new patterns I've created, while others will be old standards. You'll even find some that are very effective modifications of existing patterns. To stay within the scope of this book, we'll be able to cover only a few of the flies that *could* be used for these species (but they're all *good* ones). Some of the flies may be described under a certain section (say, sub-surface) but they may be used in other areas equally well; even a soggy dry fly will work as a nymph or wet fly at times. These little inconsistencies are what make fishing fishing. No one knows the answer (or sometimes, even the question) except the fish. The following patterns have all been consistent, tried-and-true producers, and as such are "confidence" flies for me and for many of my fishing buddies. Flies that you feel the most comfortable with are generally the best producers because you tend to fish them harder and with more concentration.

After the name of each pattern we have listed in parentheses which of the three different species the pattern is best for.

We will cover the best fishing techniques for these flies in Chapter 4, but this chapter will describe how to make some flies better fish-catchers.

Surface Patterns

There isn't anything more exciting in fishing than the surface strike. You get to see everything take place: the quiver of the fly, the pop, sometimes seeing the fish coming up to your offering, the gentle sip or the exploding water. You react with greater speed — sometimes too quickly! The adrenalin builds up as you see the take and set the hook, sometimes not knowing what's on the other end of the line. The surface strike is indeed a thrilling aspect of fly fishing, just as it is in spinning or any other type of fishing.

Even though I have been using the fly rod for over three decades, I still can't wait until it's time to fish for bluegill on the surface. Mid-spring will always find me on my favorite bluegill lake, doing what I have done all these years, taking bluegills with surface patterns.

Of all three species that we are covering in this book, none are better surface feeders than the bluegill. All the others only feed sporadically on the surface. Yellow perch will feed on a hatch of insects in ponds and lakes, but I have never seen them surface-feed in salt

An assortment of poppers.

Karen Kollmer with a pretty yellow perch.

or brackish water. Crappie will take flies off the surface in lakes also, but somewhat rarely; they usually tend to take these insects just under the surface. Have you ever noticed the little subtle dimpling at the surface on a calm lake or pond? These generally are crappie and bluegill. I have seen this happen well out in the middle of the lake in early morning and late evening on the calmest of waters. Keep a sharp lookout for this feeding situation.

What should you use when these situations occur? Usually, the first reaction is to think of poppers. These certainly do the job, sometimes, but a better choice would be a *dry fly*. Now here's a can of worms, so to speak. There are endless numbers of dry flies and probably most will work at times. Because I'm lazy (at least that's what my wife sometimes says — I call it "selective priorities"), I prefer a dry fly that can stand up to a few fish before I need to replace it with another. With this in mind, my first choice is the *Elk Hair Caddis*. This fly with its deer hair wing will hold up to numerous fish before it needs dry fly dressing or replacement. I do tie the fly a little different than most recipes describe it. Instead

Loon's "Hydrostop" will help float your dry flies all day.

of fur dubbing for the body, I substitute poly yarn. Poly yarn will float better over a longer period as it doesn't readily absorb water. By the way, a sure-fire way to prolong any fly's floating ability is to soak the fly in "Hydrostop" manufactured by Loon Products. This will impregnate the material with a silicon type floatant that will keep the fly from picking up fish slim or debris that eventually sinks the fly. After a coating of "Hydrostop" all you have to do in the field is just dry the fly on your vest, apply a little floatant, and the fly is good for many more fish. I used two brown *Elk Hair Caddis*, soaked in Hydrostop, on the Potomac at a warm-water discharge one winter, during a black stone fly hatch. I used the same two flies all day, catching maybe forty plus sunfish, bluegills and smallmouth bass. All I did was wipe the flies off and apply a dab of floatant to their undersides.

The Caddis can be tied in quite a few body colors. Favorites

FLIES AND PATTERNS

are cream, tan, olive and gray. With these four flavors you should be able to handle any hatch. Before we get into tying the Caddis, one note on working with poly yarn. The diameter of the yarn on the card is about four times too big for flies 14 to 18. The strands can easily be divided into four bundles prior to tying.

ELK HAIR CADDIS *(Crappie, Bluegill)*

Hook:	Mustad #94840 or equal, size 14 to 18
Thread:	6/0 black waxed nylon
Body:	Poly yarn
Ribbing:	Brown hackle, smaller than normal hackle for hook size. Ostrich herl will also work
Wing:	Elk hair or fine deer hair

◆ TYING INSTRUCTIONS

1. Insert hook in vise and attach thread behind hook eye and advance to the bend of the hook.

2. Cut about a 4" section of prepared poly yarn and tie down

at the bend of the hook. Leave the yarn hanging.

3. Prepare the hackle or herl and tie right in front of the yarn. Advance thread to back of hook eye and then backward about 1/16" behind the eye. This will help build up the foundation for the deer hair wing.

4. Grasp the poly yarn with a pair of hackle pliers and wind forward. Each wrap should be wrapped over about half way as you advance the yarn forward. Tie off at the thread and again advance the thread to back of the eye and back to the tie-off point.

5. Repeat step 4 with the hackle or herl. After going back and forth with the thread, leave the thread at the tie-off point of the yarn and hackle.

6. Take about a third of a pencil diameter of deer or elk body hair and place in a hair stacker, tips down. Remove the hair from the stacker and measure the length of the hair on the hook shank. The tips will be facing to the bend of the hook with the butts facing the hook eye. The hair should be as long as the length of the whole hook; cut off the butt portion hanging over the hook eye.

7. With the butt tips in line with the hook eye, pinch the bundle together while you wrap the thread around the hook shank. Take care to keep the body hair on the top of the hook shank. Do this several times to lock the hair on top.

8. Whip finish the head at this point and apply head cement. If done properly, the butts of the deer or elk hair would have flared slightly, forming the caddis head.

FLIES AND PATTERNS

Wulff fly, on left, and Kaufmann's Stimulator, on right.

As stated above, this is only one type of dry fly that will work for bluegill and crappie. Keep in mind that you are dealing with fish species that are schooling-type fish by nature, and where there is one, there probably are more.

A high floating dry fly with materials that hold up well to many fish is the best choice. Any of the Wulff-style flies or Kaufmann's Stimulator patterns will work.

Poppers are the next choice for the bluegill. Pick any yellow or white popper in size #8 or smaller with rubber legs, and you are in business. A good selection of cupped fronts and a few slider type poppers should be part of your arsenal. The Gaines Company has been producing cork poppers as long as I have been fly fishing. These are fine poppers, but a little modification will make them even better fish-catching producers. This is an easy process. Most poppers are tied with hackles tied "in the round," meaning the hackle extends 360 degrees around the hook shank. These stiff hackle fibers tend to reduce the gap of the hook, making it somewhat "weedless" to a sipping type of strike from a fish. Cutting the hackle off near the hook shank on the bottom of the hook will relieve this problem without changing the appearance of the popper from the fish's point of view (from under the water surface). The next thing that will enhance the effectiveness of the popper is to cut the rubber legs shorter. This will help in two ways. One, it will almost eliminate the rubber hackle's tendency to get caught under the hook bend, and, two, it will help keep the fish from just

FLY FISHING FOR PANFISH

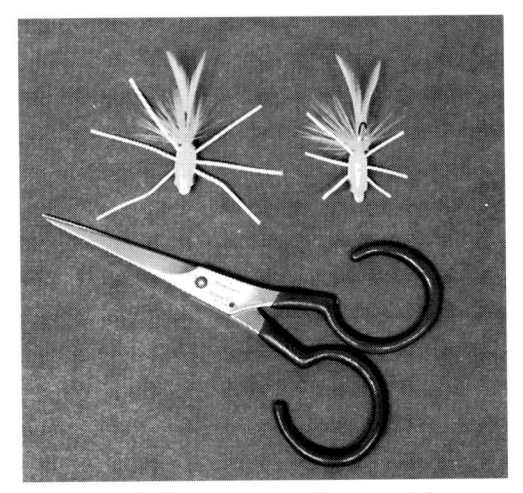

Before and after poppers. Commercial popper on left and a trimmed popper on right. Note profile from a fish's view is not changed.

grabbing the rubber legs instead of the hook. To shorten the legs, gather all the legs and pull them to the front of the hook eye. Take a pair of scissors and cut the rubber legs across about 1/8" in front of the hook eye. This will keep the legs from twisting and also give a better appearance to the popper. Each pair of legs starting from the bend of the hook will be a little shorter than the proceeding pair, with the shortest pair being nearest the hook eye.

Turtles like poppers, too. . . oops.

FLIES AND PATTERNS

    Another surface fly that will ring the bluegill's dinner bell is *Bruce's Foam Beetle.* This is tied with the bluegill's favorite color — yellow. Just as the smallmouth bass has its favorite color (which is chartreuse), bluegills find yellow the same way — irresistible. The main ingredient of this fly is a yellow closed cell foam body with grizzly hackle for legs. It is a simple, quick fly that will hold up to a load of fish without needing any repair or floatant.

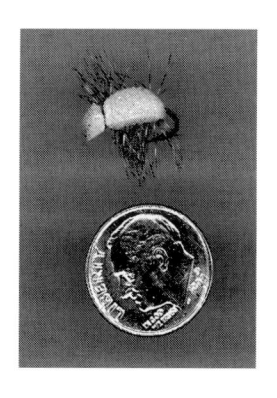

BRUCE'S FOAM BEETLE *(Bluegill)*

Hook: Mustad #94840, size 10 or 12

Thread: Red 3/0 Monocord

Body: 1/8" thick closed cell foam

Legs: Grizzly hackle

◆ TYING INSTRUCTIONS

1. Insert hook in vise, attach thread behind hook eye and advance to bend of hook and back to the tie-in point.

2. Cut a piece of foam about 3/16" wide and 2" long (if you cut the whole length of the material, use as is and use the reminder for other flies). Tie this piece in at the tie-in point of the thread. Bind the foam with spiral wraps of the thread toward the bend of the hook, taking care to keep the foam on the top of the hook shank. Leave the foam hanging.

3. Tie the grizzly hackle at this point and advance the thread to the tie-in point of the foam. Wrap the hackle to this point. Three to four wraps are fine.

4. Grasp the foam and pull over the hook shank. Take several wraps of thread around the foam and hook shank to secure. Whip finish the head.

5. Take your scissors and cut the foam about 1/8" in front of the hook eye with the scissors almost parallel with the hook shank. This will give the head a slightly slanted front.

6. Apply head cement to the threads behind the head. Take the fly out of the vise and cut all the hackle fibers under the hook shank. This will leave the hackle projecting from the side of the beetle, giving a better hook gap.

Sub-surface Patterns

The term can be misleading. What is sub-surface? It's anything not on the surface or the bottom. You might think that this would cover most of the water column in a lake or pond, but it's not really that complicated. *Most of the time, these three fish species feed and rest near the bottom.* Bluegill and crappie are on the surface only about 5% of the time, while yellow perch cannot really be considered as surface feeders at all. In large lakes and ponds the crappie and bluegill will *suspend*, meaning they will seek a temperature comfort level that might not be near the top or bottom. These fish are hard to find, and even harder to stay on once you do find them. Sometimes they will suspend over some type of bottom structure, and at these times they will usually stay in that particular spot. Another reason these fish will suspend is to feed on an insect hatch. Usually, this will happen late in the afternoon or in the evening. I have been lucky enough to catch them feeding this way many times. The next couple of flies are specifically designed to help you catch these suspended fish.

Bill Kehring shows off a nice crappie.

At times the simplest fly is the best fly. I like simple flies; they're easy to tie and they catch fish. The *Bruce's Chenille Fly* is one of these; it's extremely easy to tie and it will take panfish time after time. It uses the bluegill's favorite food color (yellow) and it can be tied faster than you can read the following instructions.

BRUCE'S CHENILLE FLY *(All Three Species)*

Hook:	Mustad #94840 dry fly hook, sizes 10 or 12
Thread:	Fire-orange flat waxed nylon
Tail:	Yellow hackle fibers
Body:	Fine yellow chenille
Hackle:	Yellow hackle

FLIES AND PATTERNS

◆ TYING INSTRUCTIONS

1. Insert hook in vise, attach thread behind hook eye and advance to bend of hook.
2. Tie a tail of about 10 to 12 yellow hackle fibers at bend of hook. The tail should be as long as the hook shank.
3. Tie in about 3" of fine yellow chenille at bend of hook and advance thread to about 1/8" behind hook eye.
4. Wind chenille to this point, tie it off and cut the tag.
5. Select a yellow hackle of a size to match the hook and tie in at the tie-off point of the chenille. Take a couple of wraps around the hook shank and tie off.
6. Finish head; whip finish and apply head cement.

As you can see, this is an easy but effective pattern for bluegill and crappie. I have tied and used this fly for over thirty years, and it has "saved my bacon" on many occasions throughout the years. The fly has almost neutral buoyancy and can be fished just under the surface with short inch-long strips when the 'gills or crappie are feeding out in the lake. This fly also seems to get the bluegills going sometimes when they are on their beds and won't take your normal offerings. Yes, sometimes bluegill *won't* bite, even when they are protecting their beds. This fly has renewed their interest more times then I can remember in such situations.

Whereas the Chenille Fly has neutral buoyancy, the next fly will create a slight jigging motion when retrieved under the surface. The *Marabou Bead-Head* uses a brass bead in back of the hook eye for a little weight. It also causes it to be "front balanced." This means that the fly will dip down at the head during the pause between strips. This is another simple fly with real fish-catching qualities. Although using beads to weight a fly has became popular in the last few years, the concept has been used in Europe for years. The *Marabou Bead-Head* can be tied in several colors: white, black, red, orange, chartreuse and, of course, yellow; all will work well at times. Crappie seem to prefer different colors at different times, so a few of each color should be carried during an outing. An extra bonus with this fly is that it works in trout streams, too. The marabou tail will drive the trout wild at times.

MARABOU BEAD-HEAD *(All Three Species)*

Hook:	Mustad #94840, sizes 8 to 12, or same size jig hook
Thread:	Fire-orange flat waxed nylon
Body:	Turkey marabou
Head:	1/8" solid brass bead

FLIES AND PATTERNS

♦ TYING INSTRUCTIONS

1. Take the hook and bend down the barb. Slide a brass bead over the hook point and push it around the bend and up the shank to the back of the hook eye.//
2. Attach the thread just behind the bead and tie in about 1/8 of a pencil thickness of marabou behind the bead. Allow the marabou to twist around the hook shank as you bind the material down.
3. At this same point, whip finish the head and apply a little head cement.

As you can see this *is* a simple fly, but don't be deceived into thinking that such simplicity won't catch fish.

Although the previous two flies are listed as sub-surface types, they can be used anywhere in the water column. In the early spring when fish aren't as active, a slow-sinking or slowly stripped fly will allow the slower moving fish time to take the fly.

Some other flies that will work well under the surface are the underrated and almost forgotten *wet flies*. These old patterns have been used for years by fly fisherman "in the know" with great success. The Royal Coachman, Light Cahill, Picket Pin and the Black Gnat are only a few of these fine fish-catching flies that don't get the notoriety that some of

A collection of wet flies.

the newer patterns get. When was the last time that you used a wooly worm? This is a wet fly. How about the old Professor? This is a fly that will take any species of panfish and, guess what? It has a yellow body (here's that favorite color again). Give this old pattern a shot — I'm sure you will be pleased with the result.

Although the original fly's body was tied with yellow silk, the better modern way is to tie the body and head with the same material — yellow flat waxed nylon. The following recipe features the use of this material.

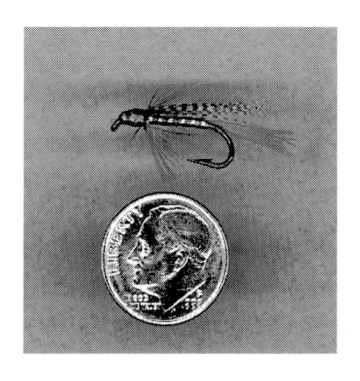

PROFESSOR WET FLY *(All Three Species)*

Hook:	Mustad #3906B, sizes 8 to 12
Thread:	Yellow flat waxed nylon
Tail:	Red duck quill or hackle fibers (preferred)
Body:	Yellow flat waxed nylon
Ribbing:	Fine flat silver tinsel
Hackle:	Ginger or brown hackle
Wing:	Natural mallard flank feather fibers
Head:	Yellow flat waxed nylon

FLIES AND PATTERNS

◆ **TYING INSTRUCTIONS**

1. Insert hook in vise and attach thread behind hook eye and advance to the bend of hook.

2. Take about 12 to 15 red hackle fibers and tie in at the bend of hook to form the tail. The fibers should extend past the hook about 3/4 of the hook shank length.

3. Tie the tinsel in at this point, and wind a wrap of thread behind the tinsel and proceed to wind the thread to a point about 1/8" behind the hook eye.

4. Rib the tinsel over the body to the hanging thread, tie off and cut tag.

5. Prepare the hackle quill, tie in and take two to three wraps around the hook shank. Tie off and cut off remaining hackle.

6. Take about twenty mallard flank feather fibers and tie in on top of hook shank over the ginger or brown wind hackle. The mallard fibers should extend slightly past the bend of the hook.

7. Form head, whip finish and apply head cement.

There you have it. The above will give you a nice little selection of flies for those difficult times when the fish are neither on top nor holding right on the bottom.

Bottom-Bouncers

Down on the bottom is where the fish eat, sleep (or at least rest) and seek shelter. This is where you should spend most of your fishing time. As stated before, most fish feed on the surface only a small percentage of the time, so maybe 90% of their lives are spent on or near the bottom, doing the three things that they need for survival. They need food (most of their forage, like crustaceans and insect nymphs, lives on the bottom), they need a place to rest, and lastly, they need an area where they can hide from predators. These are also the same reasons that the food source is there.

The following fly patterns are tried-and-true flies that will ring the panfish's dinner bell. Some patterns will work for all three species of panfish and some seem to work better with certain ones.

By far the most consistently successful fly pattern for the bottom is the *Wooly Bugger*. Also, the best color is black, but not *all* black. What do I mean by that? Have you seen many animals

A black wooly bugger and a scrappy bluegill. . . this makes fly fishing for panfish fun!

or insects that are entirely one color? This just doesn't happen very often. Maybe any food source that was all one color has long since been eaten by some predator. Lift up a small rock in a stream. Notice how all the insects that are on the bottom of the rock are multi-colored. The ones on the dark portion of the rock are dark, and the light portions of the rock support light-colored insects. They are trying to hide, and are doing their best to camouflage themselves. My point is, *don't tie any fly entirely with the same color or density of color.*

No one knows for sure what a wooly bugger represents to a fish, but it could be a minnow, leech, crawfish, hellgrammite, or other such creature. The following pattern takes this variability into consideration within the tying instructions.

Every wooly bugger that we tie in my shop is tied with grizzly hackle as the ribbing. This variegated hackle creates the illusion of movement as the hackle colors change from black to white. This effect could, for example, represent the joints in an appendage if the wooly bugger is interpreted as a crawfish or hellgrammite. Another of our tying modifications is to make the body and hackle larger at the tail than at the hook eye. This would be more in keeping with the shape of a leech, which is larger in the body and smaller at the head. The point here is that if you are tying a generalized fly pattern, try to tie it in a way that will give the impression of as many food sources as you can.

FLY FISHING FOR PANFISH

BLACK WOOLY BUGGER *(All three species)*

Hook:	Mustad #9672 — 3x streamer hook, sizes 6 to 12
Thread:	Fire-orange flat waxed nylon
Lead Wire:	.025 for #6, .015 for #8, .010 for #10 and smaller
Tail:	Black turkey flat marabou
Body:	Medium black chenille for #6 or 8 hooks and fine for #10 or smaller
Ribbing:	Grizzly saddle hackle
Head:	Fire-orange flat waxed nylon

FLIES AND PATTERNS

◆ TYING INSTRUCTIONS:

1. Insert hook in vise and attach thread behind the hook eye and wind to bend of hook.

2. Take about four inches of the proper size lead wire and wrap on the hook shank at the point above the hook point. Wind to about 3/16" behind the hook eye. By wrapping the lead in this manner the fly will tend to sink on a level plane, which is what a minnow would do; this allows the fly pattern to represent yet another food source.

3. Pull about 3/4" to 1" of marabou off one side of a turkey flat and attach behind the lead wire at the bend of the hook. Bind down the marabou as you advance the thread to the bend of the hook. The marabou should extend behind the hook the length of the entire hook.

4. Cut about 3" to 4" of chenille and tie it at this point and let it hang.

5. Prepare a grizzly saddle hackle long enough to palmer the length of the hook. Tie it in by the base, NOT the tip (this creates the "bigger-at-the-butt" shape). Advance thread to near the hook eye, ahead of the lead, and wind a slope from the lead to the hook shank. This will allow a smooth wrap of the chenille.

6. Grasp the chenille and wind one wrap behind the grizzly saddle and one in front of the hackle; continue wrapping to the thread. Tie off, cut and bind down tag.

7. Grasp the saddle hackle and palmer forward and tie off at the same point. Wind a tapered head and cement.

One of my fishing heroes when I first got into fly fishing was the late Joe Brooks. Although he fished all over the world, his home was here in Maryland where he fished for smallmouth and largemouth bass, trout and bluegill. His love for fishing encompassed just about all fish species. One of Joe's fly patterns that I first used for panfish was his *Black Lacquered Ant*.

It was tied with a thread body covered with black lacquer, and I used this tying technique for years. I also tied it with fluorescent red thread for early spring "bluegilling." It's a little heavier than neutral buoyancy, so the fly will allow the slow descent and retrieve necessary to make the cold-weather bluegills bite. Early season crappie also went for these tasty tidbits.

To make use of more modern and durable materials, I now tie the same ant, but cover the body with five minute epoxy. I renamed the modified fly the *Epoxy Ant*.

I tie this pattern in three thread colors; black, chartreuse and fire-orange. This is definitely a fly worth tying, especially in the fire-orange color. The colored thread and clear epoxy gives these flies the translucency and gloss that real ants possess. By the way, trout won't turn up their noses to these flies. They love them.

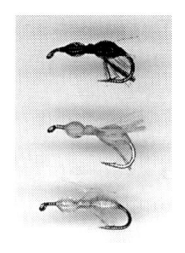

FLIES AND PATTERNS

EPOXY ANT *(Crappie, Bluegill)*

Hook: Mustad #94840 or equal, size #14 thru #18

Thread: Flat waxed nylon — black, chartreuse, fire-orange

Body: Thread

Wings: Thread or neer hair

The color of the wings are generally matched to the body, but they can be other colors if you wish.

◆   TYING INSTRUCTIONS:

   1. Place hook in vise, attach thread behind eye and advance to bend of hook.

   2. Build a longish bump for the abdomen with the thread. This body should be a third of the hook shank.

   3. Advance thread to back of hook eye and create a second, smaller bump — a few wraps will do. Finish head with a whip finish.

   4. If you used colored thread, mix some clear epoxy and apply to the two bumps. The rear bump should have

more epoxy applied to build up the body. If you need to add pigment to the epoxy to gain color, use powder paint and mix this right in the epoxy and coat the body.

5. After the epoxy has set, reinsert the hook in the vise and tie in the thread between the bodies. Do not cut the thread. Tie off thread with a whip finish and cut the thread about 3/8" long. Now cut the tag end the same length, and you have legs and wings. If you want a different color for the wing and legs, instead of using the colored thread, use fine clear monofilament and "Neer Hair" or "Fly Fur" or something similar and tie it in like you did the thread.

6. After whip finishing, add a little head cement at this junction.

Note: Applying the epoxy to a fly this small can be difficult. A simple, but effective, holder is a small electrical "Alligator Clip." Just hold the hook with the eye pointing down and, grasping the clip with the spring clip up, catch the *hook eye only* in the jaws. This will allow you to just pull the hook point into the cork on the drying motor and just let go. For speed and epoxy savings, hook up about five clips at a time; there won't be any lost time trying to get the hook eye in the jaws.

Although we've described this fly as a "bottom-bouncer," it is equally as effective when used as a sub-surface fly.

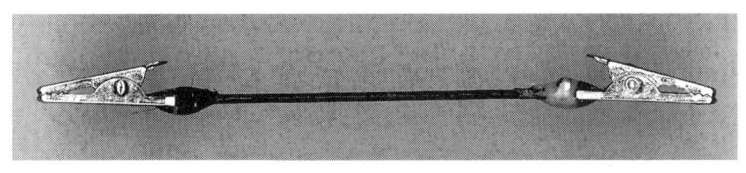

An alligator clip is a great tool to use when applying epoxy to the ant.

FLIES AND PATTERNS

The *Montana Nymph* is used as a good stonefly imitation out West, and it's a great fly for panfish in the East. Weighting this fly and sending it to the bottom with its buggy-looking profile will entice the 'gills, "specks" and "raccoon perch" to inhale this morsel for their dinner. The following pattern has a few *Fisherman's Edge* changes: grizzly hackle replaces the brown or ginger hackles, and brown chenille is used for the body in lieu of the traditional black.

MONTANA NYMPH *(All three species)*

Hook:	Mustad #9672, size 8
Thread:	Fire-orange flat waxed nylon
Tails:	Brown hackle fibers
Lead:	.015 lead wire
Body:	Medium brown chenille
Wing Case:	Medium brown chenille
Legs:	Grizzly hackle
Thorax:	Medium yellow chenille
Head:	Fire-orange flat waxed nylon

♦ **TYING INSTRUCTIONS:**

1. Insert hook in vise and attach the thread behind the hook eye and wind to bend of hook.

2. Take about 10 brown hackle fibers and tie in at the bend of hook for the tail. Hackles should extend past hook bend 1/3 hook length.

3. Wrap lead wire starting on the hook shank from a point opposite the hook point. Wrap forward to a point about 1/4" from hook eye.

4. Cut 5" of brown chenille and tie in at bend of hook. Wrap forward about 2/3 of the hook shank and tie off. Take the tag end and tie it down in the same place to form a loop in the chenille. This will be the wing case.

5. Cut 2" of yellow chenille and tie in at this point. Let it hang.

6. Prepare a grizzly hackle and tie in by the butt at the same point as the yellow chenille.

7. Grasp the yellow chenille with your hackle pliers and wind two or three turns toward the hook eye. Tie off and cut tag.

8. Grasp the grizzly saddle hackle and palmer over the yellow chenille. Two to three turns is enough. Tie off and cut tag.

9. Pull the looped brown chenille over the yellow chenille and the hackle, and tie down in back of the hook eye. Cut tag, form head and apply head cement.

FLIES AND PATTERNS

Are you familiar with the *Clouser's Deep Minnow*? This is a creation of Bob Clouser from Middletown, Pennsylvania. Bob's great love is fishing for smallmouth bass on the Susquehanna River. The Deep Minnow is to the fly fisherman what the lead head jig is to the spin fisherman. The pattern has a dumbbell shaped eye for weight, and uses different colored bucktail and tinsel for the body. Lefty Kreh states that this is one of the best underwater flies ever designed. Lefty has taken eighty plus species of fish with this fly, and he's used it all over the world.

It is also a great fly for panfish when scaled down to their size. I tie this pattern for bluegill and crappie down to size 12 on dry fly hooks. In the early spring, a blue-and-black *Mini-Clouser* does well. You need to carry a few of these patterns from size 6 to 12s in colors chartreuse-and-white, all white and the blue-and-black I mentioned. If you are familiar with tying Clouser Minnows, note that our variation ties-in the bucktail a little differently.

Captain Gary Neitzey

FLY FISHING FOR PANFISH

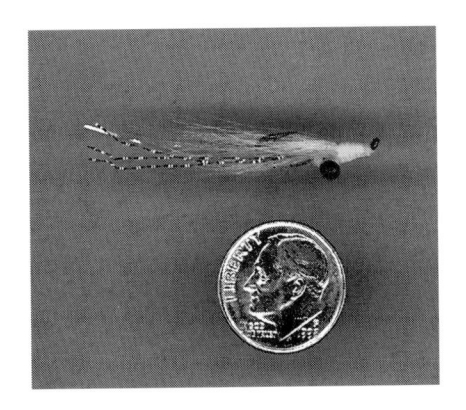

MINI PANFISH CLOUSERS *(All Three Species)*

Hook: Mustad #94840, size 6 to 12

Thread: Fire-orange flat waxed nylon

Eye: #6 & 8 Hooks — 1/50 oz lead eye

#10 & 12 — 1/100 oz lead eye

Underbody: Bucktail

Tinsel: Flashabou

Overbody: Bucktail

	Blue & Black	Chartreuse	White
Underbody	Blue Bucktail	White	White
Tinsel	Rainbow Flashabou	Pearl Flashabou	Pearl Flashabou
Overbody	Black Bucktail	Chartreuse	White

FLIES AND PATTERNS

♦ TYING INSTRUCTIONS:

1. Insert hook in vise and attach thread behind hook eye and advance back about 1/3 of hook shank.

2. Tie in lead dumbbell eye by wrapping over eye and hook shank from left to right and then right to left over eye (it makes a figure-eight pattern). After the eye is tied in tight, lash the lead eye in place by wrapping the thread under the lead eye and over the hook shank on the back and front side of the eye. Advance thread in front of the lead eye.

3. Turn hook over in vise. Cut about 7 to 10 strands of bucktail, align the tips, and measure the length over hook. The bucktail should be about 1/2 hook shank longer than the hook. Tie in just in front of the head eye and wind thread in back of lead eye and tie down bucktail at this point also. Advance thread in front of lead eye.

4. Cut 8 to 10 strands of Flashabou and tie in just in front of the bucktail tie-in point. Let the tinsel extend 1/4" past the bucktail.

5. Cut about twice the thickness of bucktail overbody as underbody and tie in right in front of the tinsel. This will allow for a thin tapered head. This bucktail should be as long as the underbody.

6. Form a smooth tapered head, whip finish and apply head cement.

I'll remind you again that these are but a few of the best fly patterns which will work well on panfish. The potential numbers are almost unlimited. Your fishing buddy probably has a favorite pattern; give it a try. When visiting the local fly shops, ask what is hot for panfish. Even though we've provided some patterns that are proven to be very successful, don't hesitate to use any source you can think of to increase your fly arsenal.

Chapter 4

FISHING TECHNIQUES

Where To Fish

Fish need three items to survive: food, shelter and a place to rest. The three panfish we have focused on can be caught in a variety of waters from small ponds and lakes to the large impoundments found around the country to brackish and saltwater. They need these three survival items in any of these waters. Let's discuss where to look.

A beaver hut is always a good place to try in cool weather.

The beavers are at it again. What makes these areas good is the deep water in front of these entrances.

Breaking down water as to where fish will be at any given time requires a little home investigation before making that first cast. Check with your fishing buddies to see if they have fished the waters you are interested in. Also, check at the local fishing shops. Most shops in the area should be able provide you with some information. Is there a topographic map or a marine chart of the bottom available? These maps are invaluable. Now where do you look? Look for *deep water close to the shore.* Such areas are prime places to investigate. What time of year is it? Early spring will have the fish in one area and late spring will have them in another. Early spring will find most of the panfish near deep water with structure. Find the deeper water and look for structure on nearby shores; this is one of the best starting points in cold weather. In ponds and lakes look for beaver huts. These huts are always on the deep water shore since beavers need the deep water to access their entrances during ice-up. The creatures are smart enough to put their entrances below the freeze line. The panfish (and the

FISHING TECHNIQUES

Never pass up stumps.

food they're after) use these areas for the main three reasons: food, shelter and a place to rest. If this type of structure isn't available in your area, then look for fallen trees sliding into the deep water; chances are there will be panfish of one or more species there.

As the waters start to warm, look for the bluegills to move to shallow flats and under overhanging trees in the backs of coves. These waters will warm first. The crappie will spread around, but will concentrate on structure near deep water. Look for stumps, rocks or logs lying on shores near deep water. Generally these areas will hold only a few crappie at a time, as they are scattering around looking for spawning areas. Crappie are not nest builders; they will fan a small depression along-side of the structure and deposit their eggs. Yellow perch will usually stage around small streams entering the lake for their spawning, which occurs a little earlier than the crappie and bluegill.

Does your water have grass on the bottom? If so, look for the panfish to be at the second weed line or "debris line." What is

Trees hanging over the water are a good place to cast toward. Insects fall from the trees, and panfish know this.

a debris line? This is a specific area in most waters that collects the twigs, leaves and grasses that become water-logged and sink to the bottom. The reason they collect where they do is because of wave action, caused by winds turning the water over. This line is usually on the side that the winds most frequently blows on a particular body of water. In tidal waters this is also caused by winds along with the effects of the tide.

Where and how far from shore do these areas exist? That is determined by the slope of the shore. In general, the slower the slope the farther from shore this line will be. This is the very reason that as you approach the shore, your first casts should not necessarily be up against the shore. Try casting several feet off from shore, and then move closer for additional casts. If you just rush to the shore, your boat might be over the best fishing in the area.

The illustration shows where the debris line is and where you should approach these areas to fish. Here's a little hint. These

FISHING TECHNIQUES

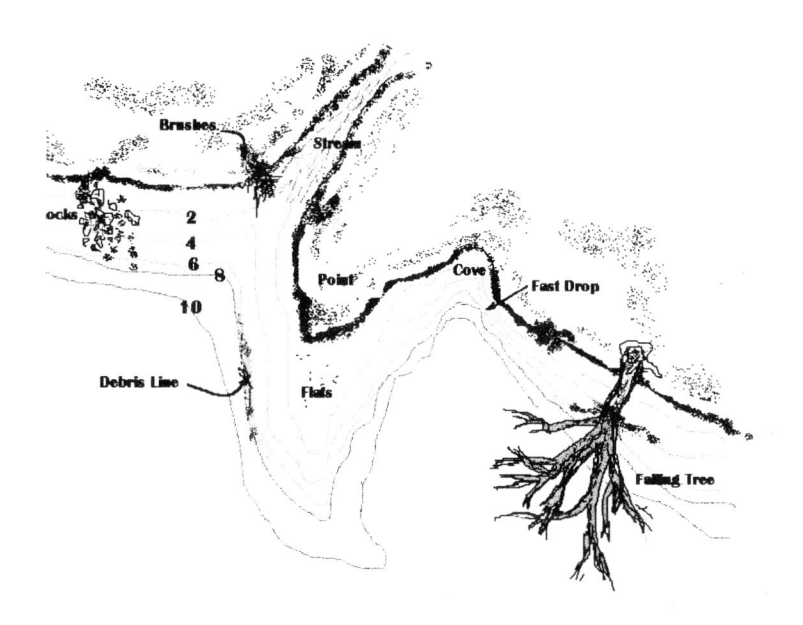

A few good areas to look for panfish. . . rock, flats, brushes overhanging the water, stream entering the lake. Those fish havens. . . the debris lines.

areas are much easier to see when the sun is high in the sky. Make a note on where and approximately how far from shore these areas exist. They are prime fishing waters as the waters start to warm, and are even more so after spawning takes place.

Many times I have found these spots in ten to twelve feet of water and had great summertime fishing when the rest of the lake was not giving up many catches because of warm weather. Most of the "bull" bluegill, after spawning, will be found in waters of about these depths.

The same situation is true in brackish or saltwater. These debris lines and secondary drops on the bottom will hold fish. There are plenty of shrimp, scuds and small minnows using these same areas for food and shelter. It stands to reason that the predatory panfish will do the same thing.

Fallen trees in the water are a panfish's haven. . . food, shelter and a place to rest. . . panfish can almost always be found here.

Tides and Brackish Water

In brackish and saltwater, the tide adds an additional element to the puzzle of where to look for fish. When there is no tide movement, you might think that there isn't a fish around, but get the tide moving and it's a different story. Where do you look? Surprise! Check out *deep water close to shore*. Find structure that is perpendicular to the tidal flow and chances are you have found a spot that will hold fish. Again, before venturing out into an unknown area, consult a chart; check when the tides are moving and ask fishing shops or friends about the water. Checking tides can be done from daily listings published in the paper or from tidal charts distributed by your State's Natural Resources or Fisheries Department.

What tides provide best fishing? There is no good answer to that question. It would depend on the conditions and location. A high tide does have one factor that I find works well. As the tide

FISHING TECHNIQUES

This is generally what's under those fallen trees. . . fiesty panfish.

recedes from shore line cover, the baitfish and shrimp also have to retreat. This allows the predatory fish a better shot at them. Another area that is good with an outgoing tide is where a small tidal pond or creek empties out into a larger body of water. This again is an ambush point for the larger fish.

Look for points and structure that disrupt the movement of the tide. Such areas will cause a back eddy, just like you're used to seeing in a stream. The bait tends to become disoriented in these areas and the predators will lie in wait for them to come by.

Points of land are also a good area to try in ponds and lakes. The tops of the points will warm first, and the panfish's food source will be the most active there. Another reason points are always a good place to fish is the proximity to deep water. The predatory fish have an ambush area as well as the comfort afforded by a deep water sanctuary. These are one of the easiest areas to find on a body of water. Simply look about you to see where the land comes to a point. What side of the point should you fish first? In lakes

Good panfish habitat.

and ponds the best side is the one that the wind is pushing up on. This blows insects and bait there, and it also offers more concealment for the predatory fish. The waves cause the light penetrating into the water to be distorted and diffused, giving the predatory fish a better opportunity to capture its quarry because it can't be seen from far off.

Surface Fishing

Of the three panfish, the bluegill is the only one that can really be called a surface feeder. Not that crappie and yellow perch won't eat off the surface, but the bluegill is king of the panfish

FISHING TECHNIQUES

Points extending out into the water are good places to look for panfish.

when it comes to surface feeding. Some feel they are the best surface feeders of all fish species, and I agree. Of the many bluegill that I have caught on poppers on any given day, very few fish missed the bug. It is amazing, with that smallish mouth, how large a bait they can inhale.

Surface action for bluegill starts around the same time that the dogwood starts to bloom. Around the Maryland area that happens sometime near the first of May. Obviously, the time will vary depending on weather, but blooming trees are an indication that some surface activity will take place.

Any yellow popper with rubber legs is irresistible to bluegills. For the subtle approach, *Bruce's Foam Beetle* will fill the bill nicely.

There isn't much magic to proper technique with poppers; just cast them out, wait a few seconds and give them a pop. Usually the strike will occur either instantly or after just a few sec-

Bill Zeller with a nice brackish water yellow perch.

onds. After you cast, always wait for the rings to disperse before you actually move the fly. Bluegill tend to slowly come up under the bug, look it over for a split second and then take in the fly.

Sometimes working poppers over spawning beds can take a little time before you can get a bluegill interested in your offering. But after the first one takes, the others are a little easier to catch. This must cause something like a feeding frenzy among the nesting fish.

An excellent time for fishing poppers is during a light rain. The rain will dislodge insects from overhanging tree branches, causing them to fall to the water. Just look around for the trees with overhanging branches and try fishing under them.

Also, the wind-blown shore can be good popper water. Wind has the same effect as rain, as it causes insects to be knocked into water. When fishing the wind-swept shore, make your cast close to the shore-line, since the insects will pile up there. If you are fishing where the wind is blowing off-shore, make your casts where the first riffles are being made by the wind. This is where the

FISHING TECHNIQUES

A nice bluegill on a popper. . . a fly fisherman's dream.

insects are going to land. During a brisk wind this can be quite a bit off shore.

Sub-surface

Once we start fishing under the surface, the crappie comes into the picture, along with the bluegill. What is sub-surface? Anywhere from just under the surface to a little way up off the bottom. In this part of the chapter we will discuss different retrieves, and talk about how to use the flies documented in the previous chapter for mid-depth fishing. Some fly patterns are considered bottom-bouncing flies, but they are equally at home in the mid-depths. One thing to remember about fish, *they will come up to a bait, but rarely will they go down to a bait.* What this means is that you can fish various depths of water with lines that might not reach the bottom (without waiting forever), but there *is* a depth in that water column where the fish *will* come up to your offering. How do you find this magic depth?

Use the *count-down method*. Let's illustrate. Say you are fishing a 10-foot sink-tip line with a sink rate of 3-1/2 inches per second, a 3-foot tippet and a black wooly bugger (I use this illustration because this is my favorite system for early spring fishing). Make your cast and count down three seconds. The line has sunk

*The rod tip should **always** be facing the fly.*

10-1/2 inches — now start your strip. If there's no strike, count down longer on the next cast before stripping. Keep doing this until you get a strike. Remember the count and simply keep making it over and over. This an extremely accurate way to find where the fish will take your offering. Of course, it goes without saying that you need to be casting to an area that you feel has fish, and where there's structure or some other key element that should harbor fish.

But this is only a part of the puzzle. What type of retrieve do you need to get that strike? Here again, a lot of things can be done to trigger a strike. The following descriptions will help you think more about the effect your retrieve has on the action of the fly. The various techniques can be used for almost any species, and have long been part of my repertoire of ways to trigger that all important strike.

First, let's look at the rod. Why is that important? *The rod should always be pointing at the fly.* For one thing, this takes the

FISHING TECHNIQUES

Hank Holland with a scrappy bluegill.

slack out of the line, allowing better hook sets. But the relationship of the rod tip to the water's surface will greatly affect the movement of the fly, as you'll see.

Back to our scenario: Using the sink-tip line, you can make the fly glide, dive, jump, quiver, swim and dance just by changing the elevation of the rod tip off the water, and by varying the type of retrieve you incorporate. This is what makes the fly rod such a deadly fishing tool. There isn't a spin or casting lure out there that can duplicate what a fly does on just one strip of the line.

Look at what happens to the fly each time that you strip the line four inches. With the fly rod tip about 4 inches off the water's surface, a 4 inch strip will cause the fly to move the four inches, but the fly will also jump and quiver. This is because the mass of the sinking line in the water will cause the rod tip to deflect toward the surface due to the pull of the line under the water. The rod will recover and jump back to its original position causing the fly to jump and twitch. Then, after all that is said and done, the fly line will move back under the rod tip because of this thing someone invented a few years ago called gravity. So on this 4" strip what does the fly do? It darts 4 inches, jumps and quivers and then slides the distance from the strip to back under the rod tip. This occurs each time you strip the line. Is there anything besides a living creature that can have that much movement in four inches? I doubt it.

Want even more movement out of the fly without making longer strips? Elevate the rod tip higher up from the surface. You can move the rod from the surface *to a point even with your waist.* Don't go any more or you will have problems with setting the hook since the rod tip is no longer pointing toward the fly. With the tip higher, you will cause more movement of the fly after the initial strip because the rod can flex deeper toward the surface, allowing more movement and longer drifts between strips.

Another point to take into consideration is the duration of the pause between strips, and also the length of the strip. These are all part of the equation that, when you solve it, will make you a better fly fisherman. *Think and experiment.* This is the winning formula for any type of fishing. Every situation is different and there is no substitution for time on the water and remembering what worked in certain situations. I have been keeping a log of my fishing trips since 1973. They are invaluable as references to the time of year, water temperatures, flies used, tactics that worked or didn't work, etc.

Visual observation is another key to the puzzle. Have you ever stopped and looked around while you were fishing, but not catching anything? Chances are great that at a time when you are

FISHING TECHNIQUES

not catching fish, there is very little activity by animals and birds alike. Bird and animal activity usually coincides with fish movement and their willingness to bite. During the day there are always periods of time when nature isn't moving. Some feel this is due to solar activity that occurs several times a day, much like the tides do. In tidal water if you have the tides moving with major solar activity, chances are that your saltwater fishing will be excellent. How do you find the solar table schedule? Check the newspapers or some of the national outdoor magazines, they often have them. Don't go overboard on technical matters, though. *The best time to fish is whenever you can spare the time to do it!*

Let's get back to the practice of observation. Let's say that you are aware that squirrels are active, birds are flying and singing, but you aren't catching fish. You need to change tactics. Whatever you are doing (or where you are fishing) isn't working — it needs to be changed. Try different flies, depths, water areas, etc. Look around; are there any heron working in the shallows? Any mid-lake bird activity? Are the swallows pitching to the water surface? These are indications that there are bait or insects on the move. If the fish's food is moving, they will be too. You need to do the same thing. Change your fishing techniques — the panfish already have.

If these guys are active and you aren't catching fish, change what you are doing.

Another fine spot. . . overhanging brush.

I can't count the times I have talked to fishermen who tell stories about the fish they caught the day before. Then they fished all day the next day, at the same spot, and they couldn't get a hit. I am always amazed that they wouldn't change their tactics from one day to the next. *Experiment; be versatile. Your fishing success will increase along with your new-found flexibility.*

Fish are flexible too. You can wear out your welcome in a particular area. The fish start seeing the same fly go by with one of their comrades on the other end, and it causes some kind of response from them. Maybe they decide they want to go for a ride too. Maybe they think, "I wonder where all my buddies have gone." Even catch and release practices will put them off. Seeing their buddies come back to the area agitated and disoriented can cause the rest of the fish to go off the bite. If this is the case, and you feel there are more fish in the area than you caught, then change flies, change tactics or change your mind. Give the area a rest and come back later when the fish have had time to settle down.

FISHING TECHNIQUES

An 11-inch crappie taken with a yellow chenille bug.

Weather will also affect the fish. Typically, before a cold front, the fish will go on a feed. The high that follows will usually mean slow fishing. In these cases *you must fish slowly and fish areas thoroughly* to get a strike. I guarantee you, panfish don't bite all of the time. They can be just as contrary as any of their larger counterparts like the largemouth bass.

One display of this orneriness is their refusal to be at the depth level you are fishing. Sometimes bluegill and crappie will suspend away from shore. During these times they are feeding on emerging insects. They will only take the insect just before the nymph hits the surface film, and they don't want it anywhere else. One solution which I have used is a technique borrowed from trout

Yellow perch love large brown or black wooly buggers.

fishermen. Take fly dressing and grease down your leader to about 6 inches before the fly. With a nymph attached, this will allow your fly to sit under the surface film when you strip the fly line. Short one-inch strips are all that are needed. Bruce's Chenille Fly works very well during these conditions.

Also, when the fish are suspended out in the lake or the pond, the "count-down method" which we've described will work. Find the right depth and just keep repeating the count. The main problem with this type of fishing is its inconsistency. The fish are generally roaming around and they don't stay in one area very long. Fortunately, this usually happens in the late afternoon or early evening at a time when the winds are diminishing, allowing you to see the slightest dimple on the surface. You can follow the fish around, casting to the rises.

Bottom-Bouncing

Down on the bottom is where the fish live and feed. Of all three panfish, the yellow perch is definitely considered a bottom dweller. Ninety percent of the time all of the panfish will be feeding near the bottom. The bottom can be in the shallows or down to 25 feet in the summer. When the fish are down at the greater depth, a fly rod is a pretty slow weapon. I would rather find some fish in shallower water near structure. As stated previously, one area to find the bottom-hugging panfish is around weed beds or debris lines. These areas hold bait in the forms of freshwater shrimp, insect larva and minnows, all of which are choice food entries on the panfish's menu.

Working these areas with a sink-tip or full-sinking line will get the fly down. Choose your line depending on water depth and structure being fished. Remember the scenario about fishing the "count-down method" with the wooly bugger? Let's look at what the different fly lines will do when you're fishing structure near the bottom. Say that we will be fishing around a fallen tree with a lot of branches under the water at five feet deep. The rest of the tree is settled in ten feet of water. As you approach this structure, cast maybe ten to twenty feet ahead of it with a ten-foot sink-tip with a sink rate of around 3-1/2" per second. The longer head will sink slowly to the bottom, and the longer length will cause it to stay near the bottom longer. You have created a greater range for your fly to stay in the best fish catching area — *near the bottom.* Remember what a line does in the water; as you strip it in, the sink-tip will tend to pull off the bottom because of the floating line pulling it up. The reason to have a longer head in deeper water is so that it won't pull up as easily.

Work your fly around the entire perimeter of the structure. Some underwater parts of the structure can be a long way from the visible part. You want to work the water thoroughly. Next, you want to fish the structure itself. You might try the 10-foot sink-tip, but you will have to strip the line rather quickly to keep it from hanging up on the branches. A better choice of lines would be a five-foot sink-tip. Although this line has a faster sink rate (about 6 inches per second), you have better control of its sink rate through your retrieve. As you strip the line, the fly will be pulled to the surface much quicker than with the longer sink-tip. The "count-down method" works over structure too. The first cast should be stripped immediately, and the succeeding casts should be counted down until you get a strike.

FISHING TECHNIQUES

Another fly that works well for panfish around structure is the *Mini Clouser Minnow*. Blue and black is my favorite. For yellow perch in tidal waters, I like the yellow and white Clouser. For yellow perch in the lakes, a #6 brown or black wooly bugger will get their attention. Fish these flies near the bottom; perch are going to spend their time there and your fly needs to be there also.

I've detailed only a few ways to catch these fish. Without getting beyond the scope of this book, we can only highlight some of the best ways panfish can be caught. Experiment, be versatile and observe your surroundings; these are the keys to becoming a good fisherman. I hope that I've got you thinking about the principles involved so that you can do your own "problem solving" on the water. Our advice, of course, actually applies to all type of fishing and fish species — not solely to panfish.

FLY FISHING FOR PANFISH

Hank Holland

A beautiful early spring morning. Let's go fishing!

Chapter 5

PANFISH THROUGH THE SEASONS

Winter

All three species of panfish can be caught in the winter, but fishing slowly is the key. The yellow perch is the best winter fish. It will go after minnows to fatten up before spawning in late February or early March. Of course, the specific time may differ in your area. Check with the local shops for this information. Sinking-tip lines fished around structure are generally the answer. Winter fishing is what I refer to as "gentleman's fishing," between 10:00 in the morning to 3:00 in the afternoon is the best time. This is the warmest part of the day, and the fish will be most active. Fish slowly and methodically, covering every inch of the structure; then do it again. Do you have a warm-water power plant around you? If so, give it a try. The EPA allows the plants to discharge water that's 20 to 25 degrees warmer than they take in. That could mean if they are pulling in 35 degree water, they are discharging 55 degree water. Where do you think the winter fish will be?

Fishing the smaller or shallower waters in the winter also makes sense. This shallow water will heat up first. Also, if the northwest side of the lake is shallow, you will probably find the winter panfish there. The northwest side of the lake receives the afternoon sun, which is at the warmest part of the day. Fish there, but fish slowly. I have fished waters like this in February and caught all three species of fish in water not a foot deep. I've also had days where I caught crappie and bluegill on an *Elk Hair Caddis* in the backs of these coves. Because of this, I never go fishing without floating line, regardless of the time of year.

Spring

Spring is the time when all creatures become active. In the sub-surface and bottom-bouncing sections of the book, I've discussed different retrieves and techniques. These all can be used in the spring. Early spring will find bluegill and crappie on structure near deep water. As the spring moves on they will start moving to the spawning waters. The bluegill will move to the back of coves and bays, and also will move to the shallows under trees and bushes where they can take advantage of insects falling from the branches. Black wooly buggers in size #8 are a sure bet, as is my yellow chenille fly. As the weather warms and the dogwood trees bloom, bluegill will start to take poppers or foam beetles. Yellow perch, in early spring, will move from their deep water haunts to the feeder streams to spawn. A #6 or #8 black or brown wooly bugger gets the nod here. As the spring warms the yellow perch will be found around the weed beds and debris lines.

Summer

Summer time is popper and dry fly time for the bluegill. The crappie will start to suspend over deeper water. They can be caught with sinking lines doing the "countdown method" with black wooly buggers or the marabou bead-head. As I've stated, these fish tend to move around so they are hard to pinpoint and stay on. One area that they will tend to stay on is around bottom structure. Stumps, logs or bottom debris will find the crappie stacked directly over the structure. Their depth will vary from day to day, but on any given day they all will suspend at the same level. This is their "comfort level." Most likely, this is the area with the most oxygen; the baitfish seek this level and the predatory fish are sure to follow. Generally the yellow perch will be near the deepest weed beds. They like cooler water.

Fall

Fall is the time for heavy feeding. All creatures (including me, in some years) are fattening up for the winter months ahead. Fish tend to feed all day at all different levels. Wherever the heaviest population of food abounds, you will find fish. Sometimes finding the fish is the hard part; they could be anywhere. They might be shallow or they could be in twenty feet of water.

Even a broken hand can't keep a dedicated panfish fly fisherman from doing his thing.

Many times in the fall I have fished full-sinking lines to get to the fish near the bottom in twelve to twenty feet of water. Again, black wooly buggers are a good choice.

Also this can be a great time for surface flies and poppers. Let the fish dictate the presentation and depth. Again during this time of year they can roam anywhere and usually will be schooled up tight. The good news is that once you find the fish, you might be able to catch them for hours.

As the weather cools more, the fish will start moving toward their winter haunts. Remember the advice we've harped on — *fish where there's deep water near shore that has structure.* Fish the "gentleman's hours", ten o'clock to three o'clock. Check out the backs of coves during this time; the fish are often there, as this water warms first.

Don't forget another piece of advice we've harped on. Fish need three items to survive: food, shelter and a place to rest, and it's up to you to figure out where they can satisfy these demands.

Conclusion

I hope the information presented in this book will help you to improve your fishing experience. As nothing is written in stone, (and I'm sure that the fish haven't read one paragraph of this book), you might have noticed that I used words like "generally" a lot. This was on purpose. Fish live in *their* world, not in ours, so they go about their everyday life with *their* agenda to meet. They need to be opportunists and take advantage of every opportunity to survive, so we can only talk in generalities about their behavior. What all this means is whenever you can go fishing go ahead and go. I know for a fact that you won't catch any fish at home, so a day out *is* a good day's fishing. Remember there is no substitute for experience. The more time you can put on the water, the greater your success will be. *Think, experiment, observe and be versatile*, but, above all, enjoy your fishing experience!

Good luck and good fishing!